Someone

By Kaeley Malmberg

Charleston, SC
www.PalmettoPublishing.com

Someone

Copyright © 2023 by Kaeley Malmberg

All rights reserved
No portion of this book may be reproduced, stored in a retrieval system, or transmitted in any form by any means–electronic, mechanical, photocopy, recording, or other–except for brief quotations in printed reviews, without prior permission of the author.

First Edition

Hardcover ISBN: 979-8-8229-1865-8
Paperback ISBN: 979-8-8229-1866-5
eBook ISBN: 979-8-8229-1867-2

Listen my little one, ere your sleepy eyes close,
To a story of someone who is small, and then grows!

A story of someone as small as can be,
A someone too tiny for your eyes to see.

A someone much smaller than this small little dot
.
A someone whose life is worth a whole lot.

Listen my little one, try and guess who
Our someone could be; I'll give you a clue.

Our someone is hiding as snug as can be,
Kept warm in a place where no eye can see.
Across a great distance our someone did roam,
Then settled down deep in a warm, safe, soft home.

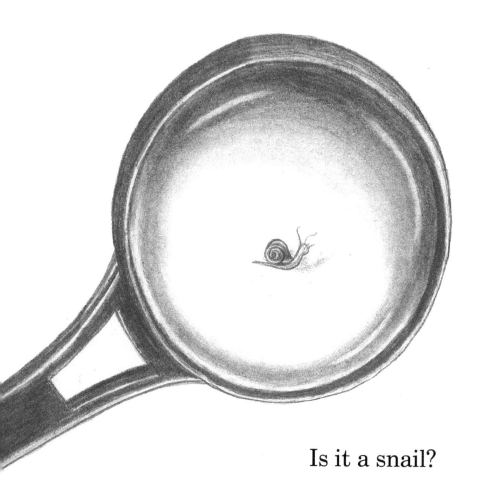

Is it a snail?

Not a snail. *In a warm, safe, **soft** home—*
Where this someone is nourished, and never alone.

Now pay careful attention—this someone grows fast!
And so much has changed since the clue you saw last.

*This teeny tiny someone
is much too small to cuddle –
And almost kind of looks like
a bunch of little bubbles.*

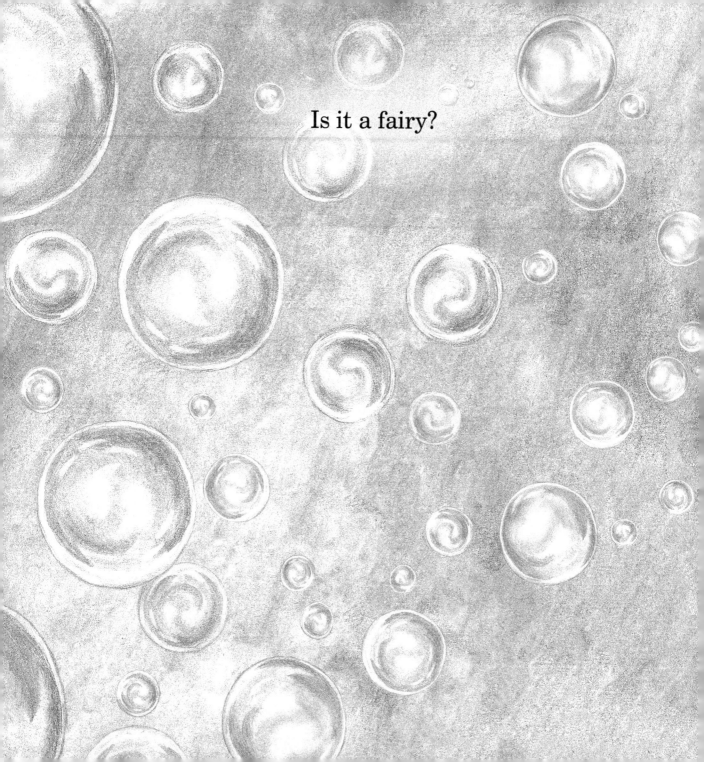

Is it a fairy?

No. Not a fairy.

Now it looks like it has a tiny little tail,
And it's just a little bigger than the head of a nail.

Is it a tadpole?

No. Not a tadpole.

*It has a heart, and a brain,
and it looks a little scary—
Now it's as big as a large raspberry.*

Is it a bumble bee?

No. Not a bumble bee.

Now it is bigger than a sweet-smelling rose,
With fingers and toes and a teeny tiny nose.

Is it a little monkey?

No. Not a little monkey.

*It kicks and it wiggles,
and it's covered in fuzz.
And now it's as large as that
great big orange was.*

A little baby bunny?

No. Not a baby bunny.

*It can yawn and taste
and hold on tight.
It's as big as the teddy
that you snuggle at night.*

Is it a baby sloth?

No. Not a baby sloth.

*With baggy skin and big bright eyes,
Our someone has reached
a much BIGGER size.*

Is it a small elephant?

NO! Not a small elephant.

Our someone is sleepy.
Our someone is smart.
Our someone is really
a work of fine art.

Is it a dragon?

No. Not a dragon.

*Our someone can smile,
can hiccup, can frown.
This someone quite likes
to be upside-down.*

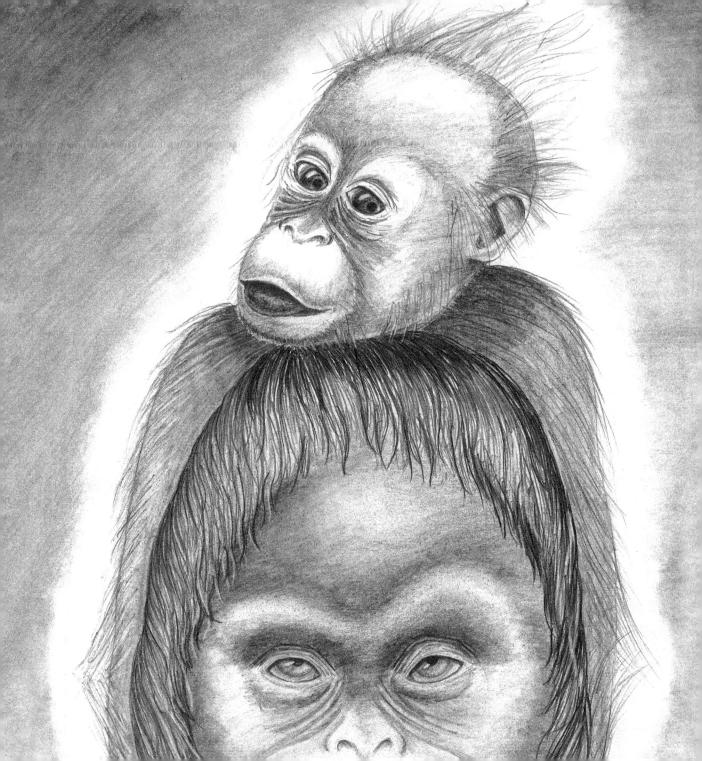

Is it an orangutan?

No. Not an orangutan.

So big and so strong, and beautiful too.
Our someone's not hiding anymore ---

PEEK-A-BOO!

*This someone began as small as a dot.
But it was always a someone, like it or not.*

Little one, have you guessed
who this someone could be?

A baby?

My dear little one, this someone is *you*.
You were small and so helpless,
and since then you grew!

In my image, my child, your body was made.
If your value you doubt, know a price has been paid.

You are someone for whom a battle was fought,
Someone whose life is worth a whole lot.

Listen my little one, hear it anew;
My life as a gift I have given for you!

I will praise thee; for I am fearfully and wonderfully made: marvellous are thy works...
Psalms 139:14

Are not two sparrows sold for a farthing? And one of them shall not fall on the ground without your Father. But the very hairs of your head are all numbered. Fear ye not therefore, ye are of more value than many sparrows.
Matthew 10:29-31

*For every dear little someone that ever was,
is, and ever will be.*

Printed in the USA
CPSIA information can be obtained
at www.ICGtesting.com
LVHW072129180823
755501LV00003B/27